# INTRODUCTION

The Gwili Railway has its origins in the Carmarthen and Cardigan Railway, established in 1853, whose broad gauge line opened between Carmarthen and Conwil Elfed stations in 1860, and on to Pencader in 1863. The through route to Aberystwyth was opened in August 1867 by the Manchester & Milford Railway, which made a junction with the earlier line 1/2 mile north of Pencader station.

Like many rural railways, the line was destined never to be financially successful, and was absorbed into the Great Western Railway in 1906. Its impecunious existence continued under GWR and subsequently British Railways ownership, and it came as no surprise when it was proposed for closure by the infamous Beeching Report. The official closure to passenger services was scheduled to take place on 22nd February 1965, but flooding at Llanilar closed the line to through services in December 1964, with buses operating the services between Strata Florida and Aberystwyth. Freight traffic continued to decline, until by 1971 just one freight train a day operated, final closure coming in 1973.

In anticipation of closure, the Teifi Valley Railway Preservation Society was formed in 1972, however this scheme foundered. It was in 1974 that a scheme was proposed for the preservation of the eight mile section between Abergwili Junction and Llanpumpsaint. The Gwili Railway Company was formed on 21st April 1975, and succeeded in purchasing the trackbed and approximately a mile of track running north from Bronwydd Arms station in September 1975. The Light Railway Order was subsequently obtained in November 1977, the first granted to a standard gauge heritage railway in Wales. The first passenger trains ran in March 1978, hence 2018 being the 40th Anniversary of passenger services, which seemed like a good reason to document the Gwili's history thus far.

However. having decided to document the history of the line, there then arose the challenge of precisely how to document that history.

Having been involved in the Gwil August 1989, I have many memories that I wanted to share, but was reliant on the photographs and anecdotes of others prior to that time.

After much deliberation I came to the conclusion that it would be too big a task to document the full history of forty years of the preserved line in the time available to write this book, but by using the wealth of photographic material which had been offered, it would be viable to produce a pictorial book showing how the Gwili had evolved over the years, with the captions providing background to the story.

As such, it is not a complete history, and it makes no claim to be. I hope that what it does do is give a flavour of that history, the struggles fought by the volunteers on a regular basis, at times just to make trains run. I hope that it is enjoyable and educational, entertaining and informative.

Other books on the Gwili, telling more of the different aspects of the railway's story, are in the early stages of preparation, and will be published as later volumes in this series. I am aware of the photographic records of other volunteers through the years, and look forward to using their images in future.

Mentioning other volumes in the series brings us to the series title "GWR Branch Lines Today" - again, we have other books in preparation, on both preserved and non-preserved branches. Anybody reading this who is inspired to contribute is invited to contact me by email at:

iain@mainlineandmaritime.co.uk

Finally, a few "thankyous" - to the photographers who have graciously made their images available for me to use; to the volunteers of the Gwili Railway who continue to defy the odds and keep the trains running; and to the friends I have made amongst those volunteers, whose friendship has kept me safe during difficult times - you know who you are.

*Iain McCall, May 2018*

Published by Mainline & Maritime Ltd
3 Broadleaze, Upper Seagry, near Chippenham, SN15 5EY
Tel: 01275 845012
www.mainlineandmaritime.co.uk
orders@mainlineandmaritime.co.uk
Trade and Retail Enquiries welcome!
Printed in the UK
ISBN: 978-1-900340-51-9

**Front Cover**

1st July 2017 was the opening day for the Abergwili Junction extension, and here MOORBARROW is pictured entering the station, having just broken the ceremonial banner.

*William Scott Artus*

**Rear Cover**

The Caerphilly Railway Society's 'Austerity' 0-6-0ST HAULWEN heads north up the bank out of Bronwydd with a morning Santa Special service on 18th December 2010.

*John Jones*

The view that greeted the would-be preservationists when they arrived on site at Bronwydd Arms in the mid-1970s. The unknown photographer showed great foresight in taking this view by recording the 'past' scene against which the progress of future 'present' images would be recorded!

*Gwili Railway Archive*

As with many formative steam railway schemes, there was a move to acquire a locomotive from Dai Woodham's scrapyard in Barry. In the Gwili's case, the selected locomotive was 7820 DINMORE MANOR, here seen being unloaded upon arrival at Bronwydd Arms on 23rd September 1979. The restoration was hindered by a lack of funds, and the locomotive left in 1983, subsequently being restored to service on the West Somerset Railway in 1995. It is now based on the Gloucestershire-Warwickshire Railway.

*P G Wright*

A pressing problem facing the fledgling Company was the acquisition of suitable rolling stock with which to operate its first services. The solution was this Class 100 DMU trailer car, then recently withdrawn by British Rail in East Anglia. This had the added advantage that the driving cab would facilitate push-pull operation - vital for a railway with no pointwork, never mind a run round loop! In this first view it is seen on 29th July 1977 in the goods yard at Carmarthen station, with repainting out of the corporate BR blue livery already underway, with the approval of local BR management - something unthinkable today.

Less than a month later, on 19th August, the vehicle is being lifted for transport in the old milk tanker loading point at Carmarthen. Note that unlike the traditional 'low loader' style of transport which is now ubiquitous today, for its move the vehicle has been separated from its bogies, which would be transported separately, and with which it would be reunited on Gwili metals.

Finally, later in August, the vehicle is seen having the repaint finished at Bronwydd Arms. The livery would later be colloquially known as "Gwili Green and Cream".

*All: John Jones*

And to haul the first carriage, a steam loco was needed. The solution was this diminutive Peckett (Works No. 1967). It is pictured here being steam tested on 22nd March 1978. The DMU trailer can be seen behind.

Four days later, the locomotive was officially named MERLIN by broadcaster Wynford Vaughan Thomas, who at the time had just presented the "Great Little Trains of Wales" television series, which had featured the Gwili in an episode on lines which had not yet been reopened. The naming was bilingual, with English on one side, and the translation MYRDDIN on the other. It is also worth noting that the Welsh for "Carmarthen" is "Caerfyrddin", meaning "Merlin's fort", making this a particularly apt name.

This 23rd July 1978 view of MERLIN at the end of its shift shows clearly the lack of siding or run round loop at Bronwydd Arms. The DMU trailer can just be glimpsed on the far right of the picture, standing at the "in use" section of the platform, distinguished by the intact fencing. One consequence of this lack of pointwork was that when new items of rolling stock arrived, they had to be unloaded in the correct order in which the item would be needed - stored vehicles were at the south end of the running line, then the service train, and at the north end the works train, which was taken up the line onto the extension in the morning before passenger services could operate on the running line.

*All: John Jones*

Another locomotive to arrive in the early days was Peckett 1903, which came to be known as LITTLE LADY. This locomotive, pictured being unloaded on 11 December 1977, never ran at the Gwili, as resources were put into the acquisition of larger locomotives more suitable for operating the railway.

A diesel locomotive acquired in the early days was this Ruston 48DS, purchased from British Benzole at Bedwas. Photos of it in this era are rare, because for the reasons explained on the previous page, when public services were operating, it and its works train were stabled north of the running line on the extension.

*Both: John Jones*

As well as locomotives and rolling stock, the infrastructure of railway operations was also in the process of being acquired. The view above shows track that had been donated by BP at Llandarcy being unloaded on 20th May 1978.

*John Jones*

This water tower arrived from Barry Docks in 1978.

*P G Wright*

The first train, MERLIN and the DMU, is pictured a few days after the opening in April 1978, approaching the original northern terminus at Cwmdwyfran.

At Cwmdwyfran, passengers had the option of alighting and spending some time at a picnic area set up in the grounds of the old mill. This area is now a private garden. Note that by the time of this 1980 view, a second coach has been acquired - we will hear more about that vehicle later.

*Both: P G Wright*

All passenger journeys start and end at Bronwydd Arms station, for 39 years the southern terminus of the restored line, but now the midpoint. As an aside, it was named after a local hostelry whose demolition to make way for a road widening scheme caused locals such angst that they raised money for a memorial plinth to be erected at the side of the widened road - the plinth is still there! Here WELSH GUARDSMAN heads north on 15th April 2017.

*William Scott Artus*

The pre-preservation departure from Bronwydd Arms was altogether more relaxed as this short goods train heads north behind an ex-Great Western Railway Pannier Tank.

*Gwili Railway Archive*

The gradient facing trains heading north out of Bronwydd is clearly visible in this view of Class 03 D2178 returning to Bronwydd with a short train on a summer Saturday in 2009.

*John Jones*

For the Annual General Meeting of the Gwili Railway Preservation Society in 2004, a "works train" photographic charter was operated behind WELSH GUARDSMAN. It is seen here rounding "Engine Shed Curve" on its way from Bronwydd to Llwyfan Cerrig.

*Author*

Visiting Great Western Railway locomotive 4566 heads south along Pentremorgan straight on 26th October 2008. This section of track was relaid with metal sleepers by British Railways, and they are still in good condition today.

*John Jones*

Another view of the 2004 AGM special, this time rounding the curve past the cement works at the top of Penybont bank.

*Author*

The site of the future Penybont station pictured prior to reconstruction in January 1978.

Thirty years later, HAULWEN passes the same spot with a Dining Train. The colour light signal which the locomotive is passing is brought into use during special events, when the Bronwydd - Danycoed single line section is split into two: Bronwydd - Llwyfan Cerrig and Llwyfan - Danycoed.

*Both: John Jones*

This view, taken from the bridge in the previous photographs, shows MERLIN with its two coach train at the short-lived Penybont station in May 1982.

*P G Wright*

Our second view of 4566 on 26th October 2008 shows it crossing the swollen River Gwili as it leaves Llwyfan Cerrig heading towards the site of the former Penybont station.

*John Jones*

All is not quite what it seems in this picture of the DMU on the approaches to Llwyfan Cerrig station - there is no driver in the near cab, and the rust on the rails tells the tale that this is the winter "closed season", and the DMU has been stabled on the running line whilst maintenance work takes place to the track in the Llwyfan Cerrig station area.

*Gwili Railway Archive*

Our final October 2008 view of 4566 shows it leaving Danycoed and heading for Llwyfan Cerrig.

*John Jones*

Before and After at Danycoed (1): The photo below of the 2004 AGM Special arriving at Danycoed shows clearly the transformation to which the site has been subjected when compared with the pre-restoration view above.

*Both: Author*

Before and After at Danycoed (2): The photographer climbed a few feet up the bank to take the image above from approximately where the platform would later be. To replicate the earlier view exactly would have required standing behind the running in board! The location can be pinpointed by the same large tree growing out from the valley side on the left in both photos.

*Both: Author*

We now return to Bronwydd Arms and prepare to head south for Abergwili, with this view of MOORBARROW having just arrived from Danycoed during the 2017 season.

*William Scott Artus*

4566 crosses the level crossing as it leaves Bronwydd with two vintage carriages in tow during a November 2008 photo charter.

*John Jones*

The siding immediately south of the level crossing at Bronwydd Arms is used for storing spare carriages away from the running line. WELSH GUARDSMAN is seen bringing the dining train out of the siding and into the platform ready for service on 21st May 2017.

MOORBARROW heads south past the line of stored vehicles in the siding on 5th May 2017.

*Both: William Scott Artus*

A short distance south of the main level crossing at Bronwydd Arms is this minor road crossing. Note the extremely poor visibility for vehicles coming down the hill in this view, prior to the restoration of passenger services.

*Author*

A consequence of this poor visibility is that the newly renovated level crossing has a proliferation of warning signs as shown here.

*William Scott Artus*

These two views show MOORBARROW heading south on the Abergwili Extension in May 2017.

*Both: William Scott Artus*

MOORBARROW makes its final approach to Abergwili Junction with a summer 2017 dining train.

*Both: William Scott Artus*

And finally MOORBARROW arrives at Abergwili Junction, completing our photographic journey along the line.

*Both: William Scott Artus*

The Gwili Railway Preservation Society has always been the main supporters' organisation for the Gwili Railway Company. It has funded many infrastructure projects over the years, from a workshop for the Motive Power Department to the toilet facilities at Llwyfan Cerrig station. On this page, we have two examples of the rolling stock purchased by the GRPS. First, RSH 0-4-0ST Works No. 7058, to become OLWEN when based on the Gwili, is seen at its pre-preservation home of Earley Power Station, Reading, on 29th December 1977. It was restored to service at the Gwili in 1986.

*John Jones*

In the late 1990s, the GRPS funded the purchase of one of these two "Dogfish" ballast wagons (the second was purchased by a private benefactor) for use on the Danycoed extension. They had their place in railway preservation history, being loaned to the Severn Valley Railway to assist in repair works following their catastrophic landslide in 2007. They were later purchased outright by the SVR.

*Author*

# GWILI VINTAGE CARRIAGE TRUST

The first vintage carriage body to arrive at the Gwili was this ex-Taff Vale Railway Brake 3rd, No. 220, which arrived on 13th November 1977. It first use was as the railway's souvenir shop until something more suitable could be provided.

*John Jones*

It left the Gwili for restoration by the pupils of Brynteg Comprehensive School, Bridgend. It returned to the Railway in October 1990 resplendent in Taff Vale Railway chocolate brown livery. Of particular note in this view of the vehicle stabled in the yard at Llwyfan Cerrig is the Blue Peter badge carried on the southern end. This was awarded by the children's television programme on the occasion of the carriage's visit to the Blue Peter studio. The restoration of the vehicle by the school won second place in the annual Transport Trust Awards in 1990.

*Author*

Eventually the vehicle came under the auspices of the Gwili Vintage Carriage Group, who repainted it into Great Western Railway livery as No. 3846. It is seen here in this new livery, again in the yard at Llwyfan Cerrig.

*Author*

Buoyed by the popularity of TVR 220 amongst passengers and volunteers, a group of volunteers formed the Gwili Vintage Carriage Group, and rescued this carriage body, Great Western Railway No. 216, from its resting place at Pentrecwrt, where it had been in use as a residence. At different times it was stored in various locations around the railway, whilst preventative maintenance was carried out to ensure it did not deteriorate further pending restoration when time and resources allowed. It is seen here at Llwyfan Cerrig, roughly on the site of the current terminus of the Miniature Railway.

To run on, this GWR four wheeled milk tanker underframe was acquired. It was overhauled on waste ground south of the level crossing gates at Bronwydd.

In the new millennium, the external restoration of the vehicle was completed (see later pages). It is seen here receiving attention to its doors outside the Carriage & Wagon Workshop on a wet day at Llwyfan Cerrig. The then terminus of the Miniature Railway can be seen in the bottom right of the picture.

*All: Author*

The visitor for the Autumn Gala in 2008 was ex-Great Western Railway 'Small Prairie' No. 4566. It is pictured on 7th November that year, hauling the two restored vintage coaches as part of a mixed train for a photo charter.

*John Jones*

In 2013, the Gwili Vintage Carriage Trust (as it had then become) became the custodians of ex-Taff Vale Railway locomotive No. 28, a part of the National Collection. Plans for its restoration have been drawn up, and preliminary work has commenced. The GVCT also owns ex-Taff Vale Railway carriages Nos. 145 and 153, and has formulated a restoration programme for all these vehicles under the "Welsh Train Project" branding.

*Author*

To provide underframes for the vintage carriage bodies, two ex-Southern Railway BY vans were acquired. The example above was delivered to the South Yard at Conwil Elfed station, then the terminus of a proposed northern extension. The building in the background is the weighbridge hut from its days as a goods yard. This vehicle did eventually give up its underframe for a vintage coach, although not one of the Gwili's collection - it is now the underframe for the ex-Barry Railway coach being restored at Hampton Loade on the Severn Valley Railway.

The second BY, pictured here at Bronwydd, was converted into a mobile workshop and storage facility for the GVCG, which purpose it still serves pending the construction of a permanent carriage shed at the Abergwili Junction site in Carmarthen.

*Both: Author*

For a period of about ten years from the late 1980s to the late 1990s, the Railway Club of Wales was key to the operation of the railway, providing a working steam loco, ROSYTH No. 1, a Mark 1 coach (SK 24843), and an enthusiastic cohort of volunteers, a number of whom who joined both the Company Board and the Society Committee. This summer view encapsulates this, with ROSYTH No. 1 leading the RCOW's coach into Llwyfan Cerrig station.

A rare item of rolling stock owned by the Railway Club of Wales was this 200hp Sentinel, SWANSEA VALE No. 1. This unique locomotive, the last survivor of its type, was steamable for a few years in the early 1990s, but not being fitted with vacuum brake equipment its use was limited to shunting duties. It is pictured on a demonstration Permanent Way train on its relaunch into traffic at the Autumn Gala in 1991. It was later fitted with steam heating equipment to be used keeping the cafe coaches at Bronwydd Arms warm during the Santa Special season.

*Both: Author*

One of two diesel locomotives owned by the Railway Club of Wales was this Ruston 48DS, which in its latter years at the railway had a removable bodywork fitted to enable it to operate as TOBY at "Thomas the Tank Engine" events. It is pictured in this guise on the loop line at Llwyfan Cerrig.

Another item of rolling stock belonging to the RCOW was this Toad brake van. The RCOW and Gwili managements had a disagreement in 1998, and thereafter their rolling stock progressively left the railway for the nearby Teifi Valley narrow gauge line, who laid a special standard gauge siding. The Club officially disbanded in 2016, with the remaining rolling stock now based on the Pontypool & Blaenavon Railway.

*Both: Author*

# VALE OF NEATH RAILWAY SOCIETY

The second South Wales preservation group to join forces with the Gwili was the Vale of Neath Railway Society, who moved from their Aberdulais site in 1991. They brought with them two unrestored steam engines, this example being 'Austerity' 0-6-0ST PAMELA. She later left the Gwili for a new home on the Vale of Glamorgan Railway at Barry Island, but is now based at the Garw Valley Railway's site at Pontycymmer.

The second steam loco was another, smaller, 0-6-0ST, SIR JOHN. As with PAMELA, this locomotive was never restored at the Gwili, and has now departed for a new home on the Pontypool & Blaenavon Railway.

*Both: Author*

Another diesel manufactured by Ruston & Hornsby to arrive at the Gwili was 88DS No. 394014. For several years, the loco was stored at Conwil Elfed, pending the availability of siding space on the main running line, however it did migrate south to Bronwydd Arms, and saw some use on shunting duties before its departure for the Llanelli and Mynydd Mawr Railway, where a full restoration is currently underway.

The arrival of the Vale of Neath Railway Society brought an added attraction to the Gwili, at least for the enthusiast community, in the form of Class 11 No. 12061 - the first ex British Railways loco to be permanently based on the line since DINMORE MANOR. Sadly, this locomotive spent most of its time on site stored at the end of one or another sidings. However, some maintenance was carried out, witness the attention being given by one of the railway's younger volunteers whilst it is stored at Llwyfan Cerrig. It is now in the care of the Heritage Shunters Trust at Peak Rail, Derbyshire.

*Both: Author*

Of the collection of wagons which arrived with the VONRS, that which has seen the most use was this Mess & Tool Van, 71. This vehicle was an important asset to the volunteers when constructing both the Danycoed and Abergwili extensions.

This 13T metal open wagon was used intermittently on photographic charters. As with several of the other ex-VONRS wagons, this vehicle later found a home on the North Yorkshire Moors Railway.

Two tar tankers also arrived from Aberdulais, one to the main running line at Bronwydd and one to the storage sidings at Conwil Elfed station. Both were scrapped in the 2000s.

*All: Author*

Another group to arrive in the 1990s was the Caerphilly Railway Society who, like the Railway Club of Wales, brought with them their Andrew Barclay 0-4-0ST, VICTORY, pictured here at Llwyfan Cerrig, awaiting the 'right away' from the guard before departing for Danycoed. The second CRS steam loco, 'Austerity' HAULWEN, was also overhauled and saw service on the Gwili in the new millennium, although it is currently awaiting overhaul.

*Mike Goodwin*

Two most useful vehicles provided by CRS were an additional 'Toad' brake van, and an ex-British Rail Class 03, D2178, which are pictured together waiting their next turn of duty during a winter work period.

*Gwili Railway Archive*

The stores vehicle for the CRS was this PMV, pictured in Bronwydd platform with external restoration in progress. Like the VONRS, the CRS and its volunteers remain on the Gwili to the present day.

*Author*

Following the expiry of the lease on their running line in 2007, the Swansea Vale Railway Society moved their equipment and rolling stock to the Gwili in 2009. Included in the collection were these three locomotives, North British 27914 (above), Peckett 0-4-0ST MOND NICKEL No. 1, and another Austerity 0-6-0ST, Works No. 3829 formerly of Lady Windsor Colliery. All photos were taken at Bronwydd in winter 2009/10.

*All: John Jones*

# STEAM LOCOMOTIVES

We begin this small selectio of the steam locomotives have been based on the Gw in the preservation era wit the first - Peckett 1967 MERLII This locomotive left the Gw in 1988, initially for a seaso long loan at the Swansea Val Railway, but never returne 'home', being sold to th Swindon & Cricklade Railwa It is now based on the Bowe Railway in the Newcastle area.

*John Jone*

The only 0-4-0ST to hav operated regular service trair to Danycoed was the Caerphill Railway Society's VICTOR pictured at the norther terminus with its maximun permitted load of two Mar 1 coaches. This locomotiv is currently stored awaitin overhaul at the Pontypool Blaenavon Railway.

*Autho*

The 0-4-0ST probably most associated with the Gwili is RSH 7058 OLWEN, owned by the Gwili Railway Preservation Society. It is pictured here crossing Bridge 9 on the southern approach to Llwyfan Cerrig station. This photo was taken in 1987, the first year of operations to Llwyfan Cerrig. The coat of red paint was part of a job lot acquired by the railway, and for a period in the late 1980s "OLWEN Red" was the colour of choice for volunteers looking to put a protective coat of paint on some spare metalwork...

*P G Wright*

On several occasions during its preservation career, OLWEN has assumed the alter ego of 1144, a long-lost sister loco once owned by the Swansea Harbour Trust but later acquired by the GWR when the latter company took over railway operations on Swansea Docks at the time of the 1923 Grouping of Britain's railways. It was first painted in this livery in 1991 to commemorate the 200th Anniversary of the Act which incorporated the Swansea Harbour Trust, and it is pictured at Bronwydd in that year. It is worth noting at this point that a number of reputable websites claim that OLWEN *is* the original 1144 - it isn't!

*Peter Nicholas*

In the 21st Century, OLWEN has spent most of its time disguised as PERCY from the "Thomas the Tank Engine" series. It is here pictured resting at Bronwydd between duties.

*Author*

One locomotive destined never to operate on the Gwili was ex-Mountain Ash colliery No. 1, a loco which features on much archive video footage of the last days of steam at Mountain Ash, being readily identifiable by its lack of dome cover. It left the Gwili for a new home at a caravan site in Lancashire, where its livery commemorates the Garstang & Knott End Railway which used to run in the area. Note from the picture below that it has regained a dome cover - for the first time since NCB days!

*Both: Author*

With the opening of the Abergwili extension, 0-6-0STs have become the standard motive power for the line. The first such loco to be restored by the Gwili, in 1990, was ex-Cynheidre Colliery 71516 WELSH GUARDSMAN. This locomotive is pictured, again on the occasion of the 2004 AGM Photographers' Special, arriving in the platform at Danycoed.

*Author*

The restoration of the Caerphilly Railway Society's 0-6-0ST HAULWEN in 2007 gave much-needed operational flexibility to the railway, as well as being a boon to photographers as the railway's first south-facing loco. It is seen here running past the bungalows at the southern end of Bronwydd village in 2008.

*John Jones*

When HAULWEN was withdrawn for a boiler overhaul at the end of the 2015 season, her place on the roster was taken by MOORBARROW, which is on long term hire from the Llangollen Railway.

*William Scott Artus*

The mainstay of diesel operations for almost a quarter of a century has been the Caerphilly Railway Society's Class 03, D2178, pictured on 16th April 2010 awaiting its next duty.

One diesel for which the next turn of duty never came was this North British diesel hydraulic, Works No. 27878. Of the same design as the British Railways D2900 series, it was sold in the new millennium to a group based on the Bo'ness & Kinneil Railway, following the disbandment of the project team who had been working on it. It is seen waiting for the low loader to transport it on its long journey north.

*Both: Author*

A new arrival on the Gwili in 2009 was this three car Class 117 Diesel Multiple Unit from the Nene Valley Railway. It took a starring role in the following year's Diesel Gala, during which it was captured on film heading north up the bank out of Bronwydd.

*John Jones*

In the years following its arrival, it was progressively repainted out of the 1980s era blue and grey, and back into its original British Railways green, complete with 'whiskers' on the ends. On 18th February 2017, it was working a Heritage Scenic Explorer service arriving back at Bronwydd Arms.

*William Scott Artus*

Prior to the arrival of the Class 03, the main diesel loco was this 0-4-0DE, a product of the Yorkshire Engine Company, informally known at the Gwili as "NELLIE", although this name was never officially applied. In this 1982 view at its pre-preservation home at the Whitehead Steelworks, Newport, it is awaiting transport to West Wales.

*John Jones*

At the Gwili, the locomotive's resemblance to the British Rail Class 02 did not go unnoticed, and it was duly repainted into BR green livery. In this view, the modifications made to be used on passenger services can be clearly seen - the structure on the cab roof is the vacuum system to work the continuous brakes, and the framework on the front steps supported the wire for the push-pull connection, there being no run round loop at the northern terminus of Penybont.

*Peter Nicholas*

By April 2006, NELLIE's days on passenger services were over - the vacuum equipment has been removed, and the push-pull facility was rendered unnecessary by the 1987 extension to Llwyfan Cerrig. The locomotive was subsequently sold to RMS Locotec, who dismantled it for spare parts.

*Author*

This view of Ruston 48 IDRIS just north of Cwmdwyfran shows the boundary between the running line acquired from BR, and the beginning of the Penybont extension - the section of track with fresh ballast is the extension.

*Gwili Railway Archive*

A larger model of Ruston shunter is this Ruston 88, ABIGAIL, pictured arriving from the Swansea Vale Railway in 2009. This locomotive is still in service at the railway.

*Peter Nicholas*

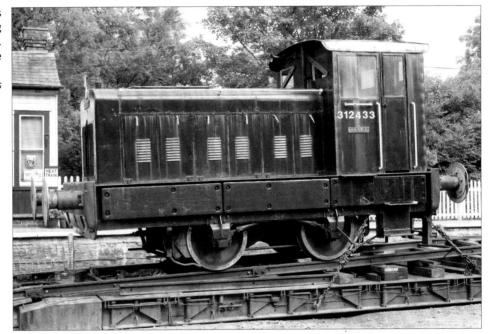

Larger still is this 165hp 0-6-0 model of Ruston, named TRECATTY after the Taylor Woodrow opencast site where it used to work. Whilst it is pictured at Bronwydd, it was later transferred to Conwil Elfed for use on the abortive extension project of the late 1980s (this extension was to be built from Conwil south to meet the existing running line at Llwyfan Cerrig). It is now at the Pontypool & Blaenavon Railway.

*Peter Nicholas*

As discussed earlier, the railway's first passenger carriage was this DMU trailer, seen here leaving Bronwydd in the 1978 season. It left the Gwili for a new home on the Swindon & Cricklade Railway, before moving on to the Mid Norfolk Railway. It has since been scrapped.

*John Jones*

The second carriage was this Mark 1 FO, which arrived in 1979. It has an interesting history, having been converted by British Rail into a classroom coach for the introduction of the TOPS computer system in 1973. At the Gwili, it was converted again, into a buffet coach, with a serving counter in place of one and a half bays of seats and a toilet compartment. Its final use at the Gwili was as a static buffet facility at Bronwydd, in which role it is seen here.

*Author*

The DMU trailer was replaced in 1990 by this Mark 1 Brake coach, seen here being shunted out of the carriage shed at Llwyfan Cerrig following a repaint in 2009.

*Gwili Railway Archive*

Not all carriages were acquired for passenger service. The Mark 1 suburban coach pictured above was one of two acquired from the RNAD depot at Trecwn, with the intention of being used as volunteer sleeping accommodation - note the somewhat precarious ladders to two of the further compartments. Its replacement, below, was a Mark 3 sleeping coach, one of many made redundant by the wholesale abandonment of sleeping services by British Rail in the 1980s. The vehicle was duly converted to include such luxuries as heating and a shower!

*Both: Author*

This vehicle was acquired with two purposes in mind, the first being to provide a catering facility at Bronwydd Arms, and the second being the ability to operate a dining train. It was a "Griddle Car", one of several converted on an experimental basis by British Rail in the late 1960s. This particular example operated between Kings Cross and Cambridge, and was reportedly very popular with the commuters on the route, but its use ended in 1980 with the demise of locomotive haulage on the Cambridge commuter trains, and it was sold to the Gwili in the same year for preservation. When its replacement entered service on the Gwili (see bottom of this page), it was sold on to the Mid Norfolk Railway at Wymondham.

*Author*

A problem with operating the Griddle Car on dining trains was that it only had windows on one side, significantly diminishing the passenger experience, which is a particular problem when operating premium services such as dining trains. When sufficient other coaches became available to operate the service trains, this standard Mark 1 TSO was refurbished and used for seating passengers on the dining trains.

*John Jones*

The kitchen in the Griddle Car had been designed by British Rail for the serving of large numbers of meals quickly, and was not designed to provide premium quality meals for a small number of passengers. the solution found was this parcels van, which was completely gutted inside, and a bespoke kitchen designed and fitted. It now forms an integral part of the dining trains.

*Author*

One of the more unusual vehicles preserved on the Gwili is this Travelling Post Office, which is displayed at Llwyfan Cerrig, and is a particularly popular exhibit with school parties. At the time of this photo, the internal restoration was complete, and the vehicle was open to visitors, but the external restoration had yet to commence.

Taken on the same day, this view shows the high quality of the internal restoration work.

As can be seen from this 2017 image, the external restoration was carried out to a similarly high standard.

*All: Author*

# WAGONS AND MISCELLANEOUS ROLLING STOCK

We begin this brief look at the Gwili's wagon and service vehicle fleet with two items that never saw service on the railway. The first is this modified "Loriot" wagon, which was rescued from Fishguard Harbour. Since leaving the Gwili it has been restored to original condition and entered the working fleet on the North Yorkshire Moors Railway.

This vehicle was unique in the UK, being a Canadian permanent way trolley known as a "speeder car", manufactured by Woodings. It spent its time at the GR stored on this short section of isolated track at Bronwydd, before a lack of progress on its restoration caused its disposal some years later.

*Both: Author*

In the early days of the railway, as with many other heritage railways around the UK, a selection of wooden bodied open wagons were acquired. The example pictured here arriving at Bronwydd in September 1977 had been donated by BP at Llandarcy.

*John Jones*

Some of these wagons were lucky enough to be restored, and were used on demonstration freight and photographic charter duties. This example is sitting with two restored covered vans on "Bridge Siding" at Llwyfan Cerrig in July 2004.

*Author*

When the Danycoed extension opened in 2001, the railway found itself chronically short of siding space, and a number of the wooden-bodied opens were disposed of at this time. The two examples in this 2005 view are seen at their new home on the Swindon & Cricklade Railway. Note that they still carry the lettering for their former owner, the Port of Bristol Authority.

*Author*

On these pages, we show the evolution of the railway's crane fleet over the years. The first rail crane was the Coles example above, which arrived from the International Nickel works at Clydach, Swansea, in 1978. It was transferred with TRECATTY to Conwil Elfed in the late 1980s to work on the extension project based there. When the extension project was abandoned, the crane remained at Conwil for several years, before eventually being scrapped on site. It is pictured shortly before meeting its end.

The Coles was replaced on the running line by this Stothert & Pitt crane, rescued from Barry Docks in 1991, which is pictured at Norden station on the Swanage Railway after disposal to that location.

*Both: Author*

When the Stothert & Pitt crane was disposed of, its replacement was this example, sourced from Stoke Gifford Permanent Way Depot on the outskirts of Bristol.

*Author*

In more recent times, many of the lighter duties of the rail crane have been taken over by this road-rail vehicle, pictured on ballast duties. It was acquired from a main line railway maintenance contractor.

*Gwili Railway Archive*

The origins of the miniature railway at Llwyfan Cerrig station go back to the Ebbw Vale Garden Festival in 1992. When the Festival closed, locomotive, rolling stock and track was moved to a temporary site at Llwyfan Cerrig for the 1993 season. It was so popular with passengers that a permanent site was found alongside the carriage shed, and it has been there ever since. Here owner / operator Fred Bond sells tickets to prospective passengers whilst the line's original steam locomotive JASON waits to depart. This photo was taken in the 1995 running season.

*Author*

As a backup to JASON, and for use on quieter days, was this four wheeled internal combustion machine, MICHAEL, seen above waiting for passengers at Llwyfan Cerrig on an archetypally quiet day in 1995. When its mechanical components became life expired, MICHAEL's bodywork found a new use at Llwyfan Cerrig, at the head of this "rake" of flower planters.

*Both: Author*

Whilst steam power, in the form of JASON, appealed to passengers, it did cause operational issues, with the need to keep steam ready for extended periods "in case". So it was logical to replace both JASON and MICHAEL with this Roanoke 0-4-0, BEN. All the locomotives were named after Fred Bond's grandchildren. Fred is seen above with BEN on the day of its arrival at Llwyfan Cerrig. During the 2017 season it was repained from its original green into this fetching shade of maroon (left).

*Both: Author*

The miniature railway is an active and popular participant in children's events at the railway. The locomotive above is a fully licensed "miniature Thomas", seen with a trainload of happy customers during the Day Out With Thomas event on 21st March 2008.

*John Jones*

This miniature tank wagon was painted in yellow "Sodor Fuels" livery, also for Day Out With Thomas events.

*Author*

We begin our look at selected stations and infrastructure along the line at the current northern terminus of Danycoed, pictured on a sunny 7th May 2008. This station was created by the preservationists at a point just south of the next river bridge, where there was sufficient width in the formation of the track bed to build a platform and run round loop.

*John Jones*

The plaque commemorating the station's opening in 2001.

*Author*

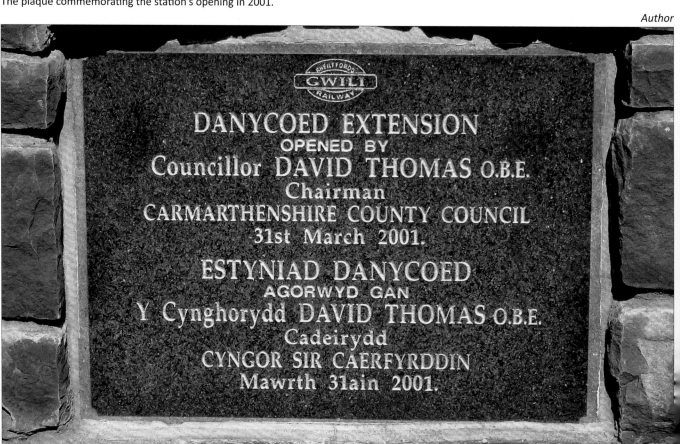

As the train enters Llwyfan Cerrig on its return from Danycoed, the first building on the platform is this diminutive structure. Formerly in use at Crundale, near Haverfordwest, as a Crossing Keeper's box, it has seen several uses at the Gwili, including as an extremely limited catering outlet, and the base for the PA announcer during special events at the station.

At the time of writing this vintage carriage body, located behind the main station building at Llwyfan Cerrig, is in the process of being converted into a buffet facility, in the same manner as the Victorian Tearooms at Bronwydd.

*Both: Author*

The original signalbox at Bronwydd Arms was demolished in the British Railways era. Its replacement is a box of identical design, relocated from Llandybie on the Central Wales line. Note the 'S' and 'T' plates on the front of the box - in the days of the Great Western Railway, these were used to indicate to travelling fitters whether the signalbox's Signalling or Telegraph equipment required attention. With typical Gwili humour, these have been set to display that the (perfectly functioning) Signalling equipment is defective, and the (non-existent) Telegraph equipment is working perfectly!

*John Jones*

The interior of the signalbox has been restored to a similarly high standard.

*William Scott Artus*

Like the signalbox, the station building at Bronwydd was demolished by British Railways. The replacement building has been constructed by the preservationists using components from Ammanford Town station building and Llandovery signal box to create a close replica of the original.

*John Jones*

The buffet carriages that previously provided catering facilities at Bronwydd Arms (see earlier chapter), have been replaced by these two ex-Taff Vale Railway carriages, which are under the care of the Gwili Vintage Carriage Group.

*Author*

# VISITORS

For the railway's 10th Anniversary in 1988, the railway hired two ex Great Western Railway locomotives - the first to operate on the preserved line. The first to arrive was Pannier Tank 7752 from the Birmingham Railway Museum. It was followed later in the year by 7828 ODNEY MANOR.

*Gwili Railway Archive*

Buoyed by the popularity amongst passengers and volunteers of the 1988 visitors, the railway hired 'Prairie' 4566 from the Severn Valley Railway for the 1989 season. It is seen here departing Llwyfan Cerrig.

*P G Wright*

7828 ODNEY MANOR arrived on the railway in time for the Preservation Society's Annual General Meeting in May 1988, and was used to operate a special train in connection with the event. Note that the newly-restored engine has not had its nameplates refitted at this time, and also the group of volunteers riding "Indian style" in the tender.

ODNEY MANOR is now based on the West Somerset Railway, and is pictured outside the sheds at Minehead during the October 2013 Gala.

*Both: Author*

An epic photo charter that lives long in the memory of all involved was that featuring ex-GWR 0-6-0PT 1369 on its winter 2000 visit to the railway. The ensuing photographs gained much publicity for the line in the railway press, being operated in temperatures well below zero, yet in perfect lighting conditions. In this view the ensemble is passing the gallery of photographers at the north end of the station area at Bronwydd.

*Dewi Jones*

Just one of the stunning images captured on camera that day. Your author was the Guard for this train, it was unquestionably the coldest I have ever been on a heritage railway - three shirts and two pairs of trousers provided little warmth when the majority of the day was spent on the verandah of the 'Toad' brake van!

*John Jones*

The weather for the visit of 'Prairie' 5541 was distinctly autumnal, as evidenced by this image of it operating a Dining Train at Llwyfan Cerrig. Note the Griddle Car marshalled immediately behind the loco.

This 2017 view in rather better weather shows the locomotive on Driver Experience duties at Parkend on the Dean Forest Railway, its home base.

*Both: Author*

The visitor to the September 2004 Gala was Pannier Tank 6430, seen here loaded up ready to return home. A GWR auto-trailer was also hired in for this event.

*Mike Goodwin*

In spring 2001, the only LMS loco to visit the line to date, Ivatt tank 41312, was hired in to open the Danycoed extension. It is pictured here with the opening special.

*Gwili Railway Archive*

Diesel locomotives have also been hired in on occasions. For a Diesel Gala in 2010, Network South East liveried Class 08 08631 was brought in from the Mid Norfolk Railway. It did make a few forays up the line, but spent most of its time during the event giving brake van rides within the station area at Bronwydd Arms.

Prior to the 2011 season, concerns about the health of the Class 03, and its ability to haul dining trains in the event of the failure of a steam loco, led to the hiring in of modified Class 14 14901. As a standby / emergency loco, it saw little use, and is pictured here on shed at Bronwydd.

*Both: Author*

In June 1993, 0-6-0PT BROOKFIELD was transferred by its owners from the Pontypool & Blaenavon Railway to the Mangapps Farm Railway Museum in Essex, where their other locomotive was based. En route, it visited the Summer Gala at the Gwili, and also the Foxfield Railway. It is pictured here departing Bronwydd on 7th June 1993.

*John Jones*

Another industrial locomotive to have visited the Gwili was JENNIFER, which spent the summer 2011 season on the line. It is pictured passing the site of the former Penybont station on 2nd August 2011.

*Phil Budd*

Like JENNIFER, 'Austerity' 0-6-0ST 68011 ERROL LONSDALE also spent an extended period on loan to the Gwili to provide cover for the 'home fleet' of steam locos. Here it heads north from Bronwydd with a service train.

*Gwili Railway Archive*

At the time of its hire to the Gwili, ERROL LONSDALE was based on the South Devon Railway at Buckfastleigh. It has since been exported, and is now based at Stoomcentrum Maldegem in Belgium, and carried War Department livery as WD196. At their May Gala in 2018, the Stoomcentrum held a World War One themed event, during which the loco is seen pulling in to Eeklo Oostveld carrying an appropriate headboard.

*Kevin Hoggett*

Extensive reference was made in the previous chapter to visiting locomotives for Steam Galas, and this will not be duplicated here. Representing this particular species of event is this image of 6430 and autocoach waiting to depart Danycoed in September 2004.

*Gwili Railway Archive*

Back in October 1990, the arrival that year of the Brake Second Coach had given the Gwili its first dedicated area on the train for parcels, and it was decided to make this the feature of the Gala, with this vintage Royal Mail van visiting, and parcels being transferred between van and train.

*Author*

Two more views from the August 2010 Diesel Gala, beginning with D9521, visiting from the Dean Forest Railway, setting off from Bronwydd. This class of locomotive was nicknamed "Teddy Bears" by enthusiasts, hence the "Teddy Bear on Tour" headboard. 08631 waits with its brake van in the siding.

The star attraction of the event was the three locomotives, resident Class 03 D2178, and visiting 08631 and D9521, triple heading a service train to Danycoed. It is believed that this is the first, and to date only, time that a triple headed train has operated on the railway.

*Both: John Jones*

Ex-LMS 2-6-2T No. 41312 was hired in to perform the honours at the opening of the Danycoed extension in 2001. Here it is breaking the banner at the entrance to the station area at Danycoed with the inaugural train.

Photographic charters are an important means of raising the funds necessary to pay for the hire of visiting locomotives, and that featuring 41312 was the first such charter to operate north of Llwyfan Cerrig on the Danycoed extension.

*Both: Gwili Railway Archive*

For the opening of the southern extension to Abergwili Junction on 1st July 2017, MOORBARROW, currently on long term hire from the Llangollen Railway, was chosen to break the banner. It is pictured being prepared with an appropriate headboard prior to departure from Danycoed with the inaugural train.

The same train breaks the banner at the entrance to the station area at Abergwili Junction.

*Both: William Scott Artus*

Gwili locos have also gone out on hire to other railways for their Gala Weekends. OLWEN is seen carrying British Railways black livery in its 1144 alter ego giving brake van rides at Gotherington on the Gloucestershire Warwickshire Railway.

*John Jones*

The Whitsun Bank Holiday Weekend in 2008 saw the operation of an "Ivor the Engine" Weekend, and here the star of the show leaves Bronwydd.
*John Jones*

Pushing IVOR close for "star attraction" status was Idris the Dragon, who spent the weekend at the miniature railway at Llwyfan Cerrig.
*Gwili Railway Archive*

The first "Thomas" event at the Gwili was held in 1998, and they became an important part of the calendar, much appreciated by regular customers. On this page we see three of the home fleet operating in support of the famous blue engine - from the top: D2178, the DMU and HAULWEN.

*All: Author*

No reference to the "Thomas" events would be complete without an image of the Really Useful Engine himself, whilst his friend PERCY has had an accident with a washing line as part of the entertainment...

*Both: Author*

# FUTURE PROJECTS

At the southern end of the line, this view emphasises the wide open space at the recently opened Abergwili Junction station - passenger facilities will be added here as and when time and resources are available to build them.

*William Scott Artus*

At the northern end of the running line, the way ahead is blocked by this missing bridge immediately north of the buffer stops at Danycoed. There are a further two river bridges between this point and Conwil Elfed station, and three more between Conwil Elfed and the eventual northern terminus at Llanpumpsaint.

*Author*

The future northern terminus of the Gwili Railway will be at Llanpumpsaint, a full eight miles from Abergwili Junction.

*Gwili Railway Archive*

In the mid 1990s, the station area at Llanpumpsaint was cleared. The building in the background, the old Farmers' Co-Operative, can just be seen in the upper photograph behind and to the left of the signalbox.

*Author*

By the time of this 2008 view, the growth of nature made replicating a 'past' view impossible, so the photographer has taken this image from a little way further south, across the road bridge immediately south of the station. The distinctive roofline of the Farmers' Co-Operative can still be discerned, poking out above the vegetation, just to the left of the large tree in the centre of the picture.

*John Jones*

Of course, as well as extending the running line, the list of future projects includes locomotives and rolling stock. This 'Austerity' arrived on site with the Swansea Vale Railway Society.

*John Jones*

Another ex-SwVRS locomotive awaiting its turn in the restoration queue is MOND NICKEL No. 1, pictured arriving at the Gwili.

*Peter Nicholas*

A project which is already up and running under the leadership of the Gwili Vintage Carriage Trust is the restoration of ex-Taff Vale Railway No. 28, the last Welsh-built standard gauge steam locomotive, and a part of the National Collection.

*William Scott Artus*

The Gwili Vintage Carriage Trust are also restoring a number of vintage carriage bodies, as part of a wider initiative titled the Welsh Train Project.

*Author*

**IF YOU HAVE ENJOYED THIS BOOK, AND WOULD LIKE TO BECOME MORE INVOLVED, WHY NOT JOIN THE GWILI RAILWAY PRESERVATION SOCIETY?**

**gwili-railway.co.uk/enthusiasts/ gwili-railway-preservation-society**